This Naughty
Love Notes
Coupon Book
Belongs To

_____

_____

_____

Thank you for buying
"*100 Naughty Love Notes for Couples From Her to Him*".

We appreciate your opinion and we kindly request you to leave an honest review in the Customer Review section. We hope others can benefit from your experience.

If you have any suggestions for improving this book or for permissions and inquiries, please send us an email at carmenancakdp@gmail.com.

If you would love a **freebie**, please send us an email with your purchase title. You will receive a printable version of the pair of this coupon book.

I love you to the bedroom and back.

Don't bite your lip. I want to do that.

Your farts stink, but until they kill me I still love you.

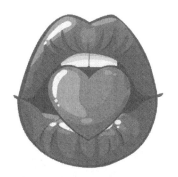

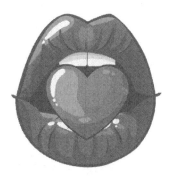

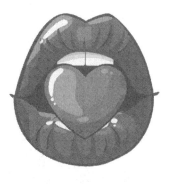

We were only
supposed to be
a one night stand.

love

I love your penis!

P.S. I love you as well.

Thanks for
all the orgasms.

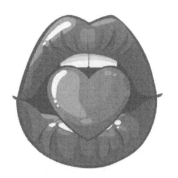

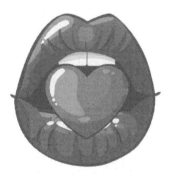

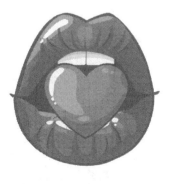

I love fucking you!
Oops! I mean
I fucking love you!

You're the fucking best. You're also the best at fucking.

I wanna feel you.
Taste you.
Touch you.

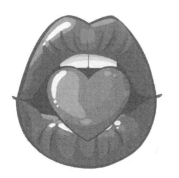

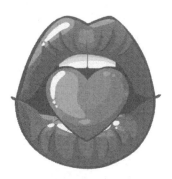

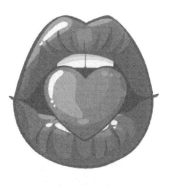

I love you with
all my vagina!

Allowing you into my
vagina: best
decision ever!

I licked it,
so it's mine!

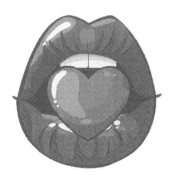

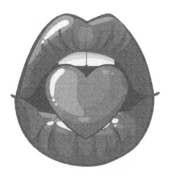

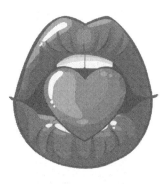

My vagina is your present.

This pussy isn't going to lick itself.

You got me dickmatized.

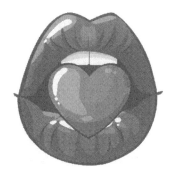

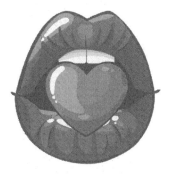

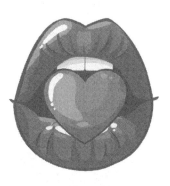

I like you how I like my coffee: every morning inside me.

I think I'll keep you. And not just because you really know how to use your penis.

I love you for your personality, but that dick is a really nice bonus.

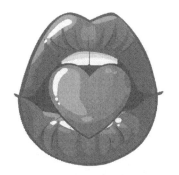

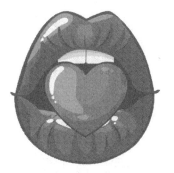

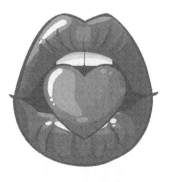

I fucking love your cock.

Hope your birthday is as good as your dick.

I'm just a girl... totally in love with a guy... who happens to have the best cock ever.

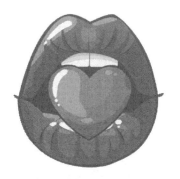

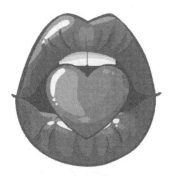

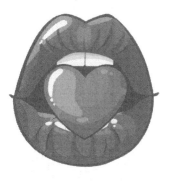

Fill me up! I'm a naughty burrito.

I love every bone in your body, but there's one I'm particularly fond of it.

I love you with all my boobies. I would say heart, but my boobies are bigger.

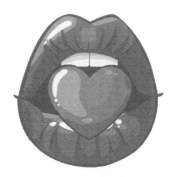

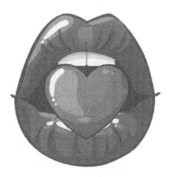

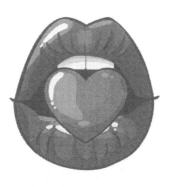

I love the way

you taste

my pussy

I hope your

day is as nice

as my butt.

You make

my ovaries explode!

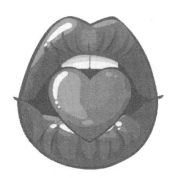

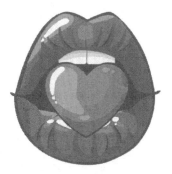

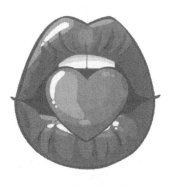

Hope your day
is as magical
as my pussy.

My vagina called!
She wants you back!

You're the best thing
that's ever happened
to my vagina!

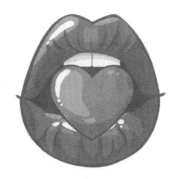

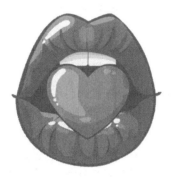

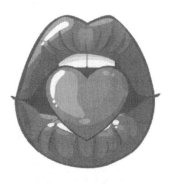

I'm smiling from ear to ear thinking about last night. 🖤🖤

Your penis and my vagina are best friends!

You..., me..., skin to skin. 🖤 Love that feeling.

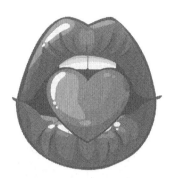

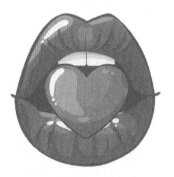

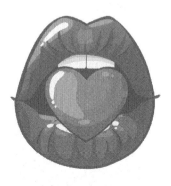

 *You are my missing piece.*

I've found your happy places!

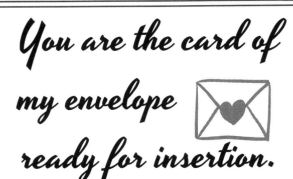

You are the card of my envelope ready for insertion.

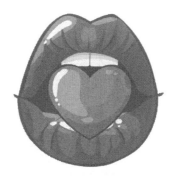

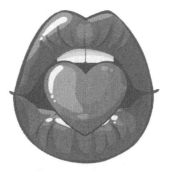

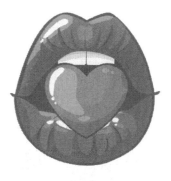

I really need you to take care of my vagina.

Wish you were here. (And in me!)

You feel so good... inside of me

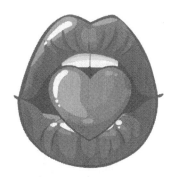

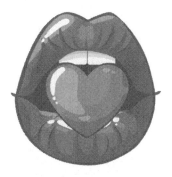

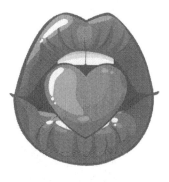

You are so naked in my head right now...

You own my heart.

And my ass

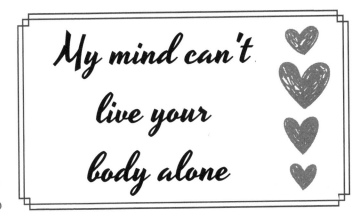

My mind can't live your body alone

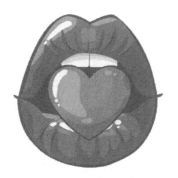

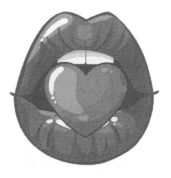

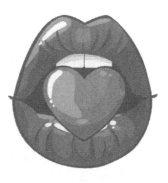

Baby, your pleasure is my priority.

I promise to always be by your side. *Or under you. Or on top.*

Spank me! Trust me, I deserve it!

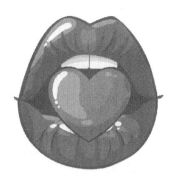

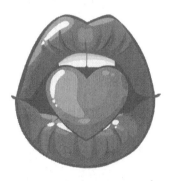

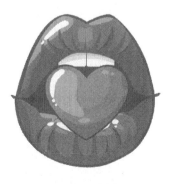

I know you wanna see me naked.

My ideal body weight is yours on mine.

I need you inside me NOW!

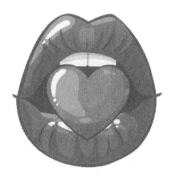

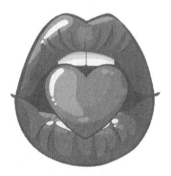

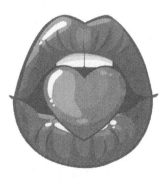

You make me
horny as fuck.
And I love it!

I can't stop
daydreaming about
your cock!

I'd like a good
licking, please!

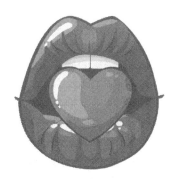

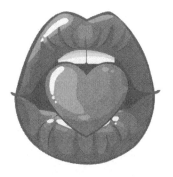

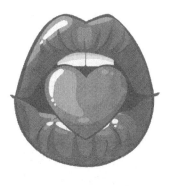

I suck in bed.
I also
lick and bite.

I love the way you
look at me when
you're horny.

LOVE

Wish you were here,
next to me.
Naked, of course.

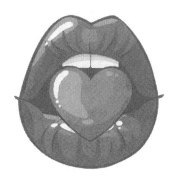

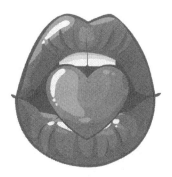

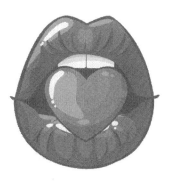

I'm not always a cunt. Sometimes I'm asleep.

I wish you would slip into something more comfortable...
Like my pussy.

Maybe making out for a few minutes would help us figure things out.

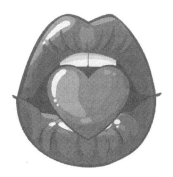

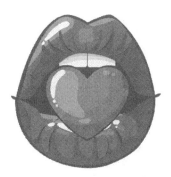

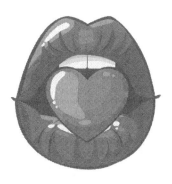

Excuse me, why are you so sexy?

That "I missed you" sex is always worth the wait!

Act like a gentleman, but fuck me like an animal.

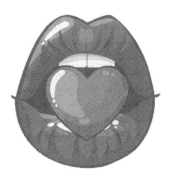

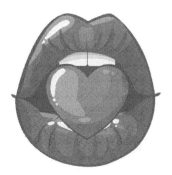

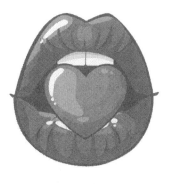

You're my favorite bad habit.

Grab my ass in front of guys who want me.

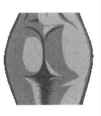

Grab my ass in front of girls who want you.

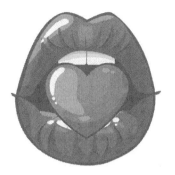

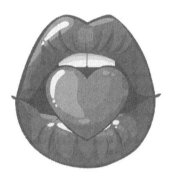

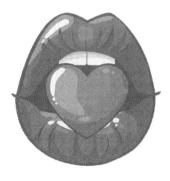

You make
my kitty purr.

A gentleman knows
it is good manners
to eat pussy.

Fuck me senseless.

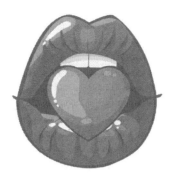

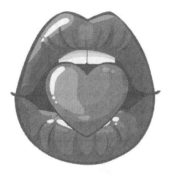

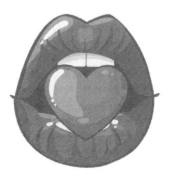

I think you are suffering from a lack of vitamin ME.

I want to cuddle with you. Naked.

I want to be naughty with you for the rest of my life.

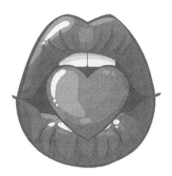

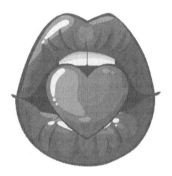

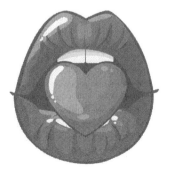

You should pretend
my legs are
made of butter and
spread them.

Those are nice
pants. Mind if I
test the zipper?

Lick me
'till ice-cream.

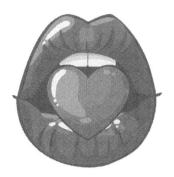

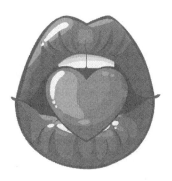

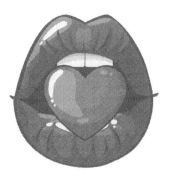

I need vitamin U.

I would love to taste you.

I fell in love with the way you touched me without using your hands.

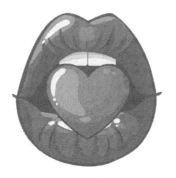

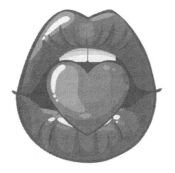

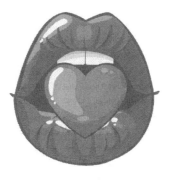

May I suggest...
That we fuck for
hours today?

I want you

in my mouth.

I love to tease

you and drive

you wild.

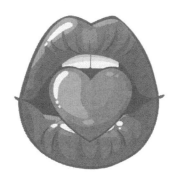

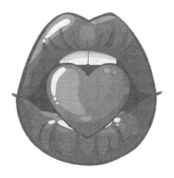

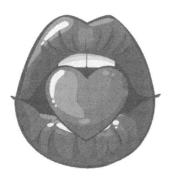

I want your body on top of mine.

Roses are red, violets are fine, you be the 6, I'll be the 9.

There's something about you that's so fucking addictive.

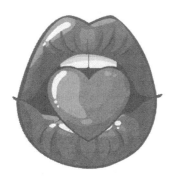

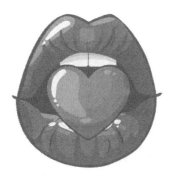

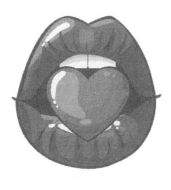

I give you permission to wake me up if you get horny.

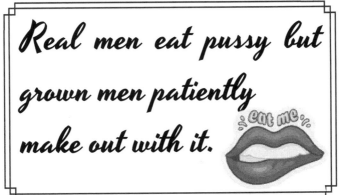

Real men eat pussy but grown men patiently make out with it.

I love it when you fuck me baby.

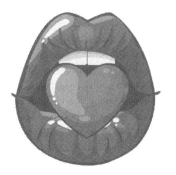

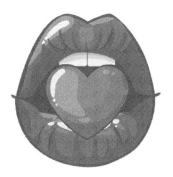

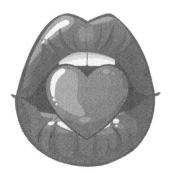

I can't stop thinking about your lips on mine.

Stress a little less. Fuck a little more.

Make me laugh, then make me moan.

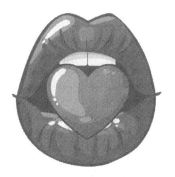

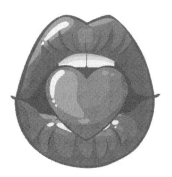

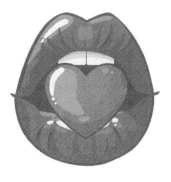

A day with you in bed is a perfect day.

Weekend mood: orgasms. A lot of orgasms.

Get in bed and play with me.

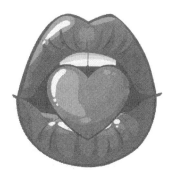

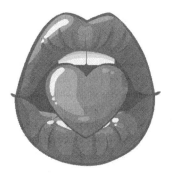

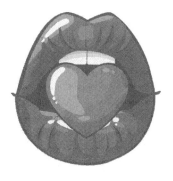

Kissing you gets me tingling in all  the right places.

Spank me. It's the only way I learn.

I deserved sex today,  but whatever.

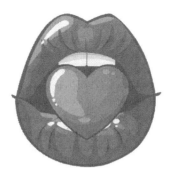

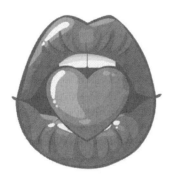

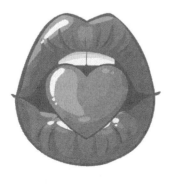

You are without a doubt the sexiest thing that ever happen to me.

My mouth wants to do sexy things to you!

I want you in my bed and between my legs.

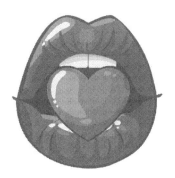

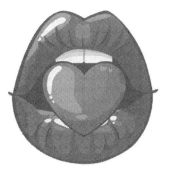

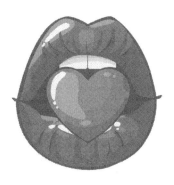

I think we should do something that makes us moan.

I love it when you give me a hug. Naked.

If you could read my mind, you'd be having an orgasm.

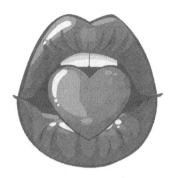

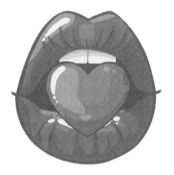

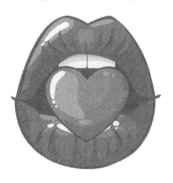

I want to be the

reason you love

sex.

Write your message below.

Write your message below.

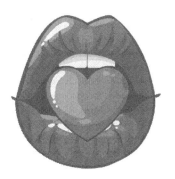

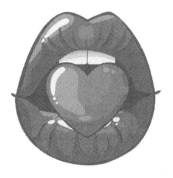

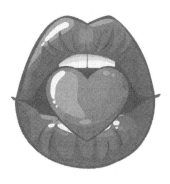

45447350R00039